'*Animal Voices* by Suli Autagavaia is a touching collection of letters from the perspective of animals. Delicately written, compassionately spoken, this is a book I will be sharing with all of my friends and networks for many years to come. Thank you Suli!

KATHY DIVINE, author of *Plant Powered Women* and *Plant Powered Men* and founder and editor of *Australian Vegans Journal*

'Guaranteed to touch your heart and help you empathise with the plight of so many misunderstood animals whose voices go unheard, this book, written from the animal's perspective, is a necessary addition to any animal lover's library.

JAMES ASPEY, Vegan Animal Rights Activist and lecturer

ANIMAL VOICES

Letters from their hearts to yours

SULI AUTAGAVAIA

ISBN: 978-0-473-49512-1

978-0-473-49513-8 (ePub)

978-0-473-49514-5 (PDF)

This is for you, Lucky, my canine son, friend and protector. Forever in my heart.

FOREWORD

As a therapist, I am no stranger to pain and over the decades I've heard countless stories of people's despair and trauma. The reasons vary as to why people seek my help, although their pain has some common threads. Whether a relationship breakup, the death of a loved one, family tragedy, mind-numbing work, fear of the future, or a lack of belonging, the common thread is, "I'm not good enough." This leads people on a path to increase their sense of worth and many fall prey to society's promise of satisfaction at the end of the consumer rainbow. People busy themselves in the pursuit of happiness, yet the more people focus on their own suffering, the further they seem to go from developing a lasting sense of meaning and purpose. It seems that I have never seen anyone truly content until they do something for others, beyond their own needs and desires.

A different breed of client has approached me in recent years, whose pain is related to the suffering of others. These individuals are deeply concerned about the state of the world, human oppression, social and economic inequities, prejudice, corporate greed and its consequences for people, the environment, and animals. Many of these clients are vegans and suffer a specific form of despair: vystopia. Vystopia is the anguish of knowing about the systematised cruelty towards animals and the trance-like collusion of society in a dystopian reality, that some are not even aware they are part of. When these vystopians, their hearts torn apart with the burden of knowing, try to share the plight of their sentient non-human cousins, they're often met with resistance. Some refuse to come alongside the suffering of animals, others disbelieve the messenger, and still others ask why they are not more concerned about human suffering. These brave individuals, who are deeply empathic to the animals' pain, look for ways to break through other people's trances and stop financing animal abuse through their consumer choices.

For those of us who have personally witnessed the horrors of the slaughterhouse, the animal testing lab, the puppy mill, or the torture of animals in entertainment, we long for ways to get others to see the animal's plight. Through human words, we try to convey the agony animals feel as their babies, freedom, and own lives are ripped from them for human use. When we fail in this endeavour, we often become depressed, hopeless, and misanthropic towards our fellow humans. Yet the animals need us to keep speaking out to end their oppression. We cry, "If only you could experience for one minute with your eyes what these tortured souls endure with their bodies, you would stop financing these industries and help us in emptying all cages."

Suli's essays have provided us with a new way to reach the hearts of those who seem impervious to empathising with animal suffering. Through the eyes of animals caught in a cycle of pain and despair in the industrialised process, she tells their stories. Her words are lyrical as she introduces us to these animals' lives in ways that preserve their dignity, majesty, and yearning to live their own lives

8

free from pain and suffering. I believe that these essays provide vegans with a powerful tool to invite our fellow humans to empathise with animal suffering. In doing so, they will unknowingly be opening their hearts to journey down a path I believe is essential in leading a meaningful life — doing something beyond our own interests to help others be free from suffering.

Thank you Suli for this extraordinary book. The animals will thank you for your courage in writing it, and society will owe you a debt they can never hope to repay.

CLARE MANN

Vegan Psychologist and Author of Vystopia: The Anguish of Being Vegan in a Non Vegan World

PROLOGUE

But if these beings guard you, they do so because they have been summoned by your prayers.

—Saint Ambrose

I stand on the other side of the gate, where I've yearned to be for so long. Free. The wind swirls clusters of dust into the air and onto my face. There is a breath inside the wind. I am free, no longer invisible. I stare down the long, dusty road to the sheds. A lonely, desperate figure is racing up the path to the gate. Sensing freedom but unable to open it, she lingers there, thumping her head against the latch, wailing in defeat. So close, yet so far.

The wired-fenced road is flanked by gentle, rolling hills of ash soils, and healthy green pastures. Despite the serenity of its park-like surrounds, the sheds house a turbulent secret. A darkness hidden from a busy, uncaring world. Fuck the farm life. There's no love or light here. Slavery is legal and flourishes on the farm. It's a bloody hard way to live. I glare at the steel sheds where the powerless live and labour without an end in sight, then 500 metres to the left, I squint with flared nostrils at the antique-white bungalow where the powerful live in self-righteous comfort.

All our lives are dictated by the rising and setting of the

sun and the transitions through each season. The sun rises, lighting up the tree tops and sweeping across the pastures, heralding another day of toil, before finally sinking down behind the sheds to a sigh of comatose relief. We work like bees on a mission to sustain the Farmer Queen. We reproduce and bear our breathing fruits throughout the winter and spring, just in time for the new summer pastures to fatten us up again for the next round of reproduction. For others, it's a continuous cycle of service with no breaks.

No down-time. No off-season.

No relief.

The days and seasons and landscapes continuously change, but our lives remain the same. Living mindlessly, floating from one command to another, is the farm life. A life under the command of the patriarchy.

I am female, I am mother, I am worker. I am all of these but none of them. Identity and self-determination are privileges that were not afforded to me. I had a voice yet I was permanently on mute. Our voice could only be heard through the heart and souls of angels. Our voice was of pain. The pain of not being allowed to grow old; to live a complete cycle like the days and seasons that arrive and depart. This was my life. I was stuck right in middle of an inhumane culture. Unable to escape to greener pastures or calmer waters has shattered my spirit.

But the trees whispered hope. The trees lifted me daily, calling me to stay, to live. They understood our tortured souls and how our painful fate would finally fade into death. The trees would bid us farewell as their branches emptied before their long, cold sleep. They awoke renewed amongst the flowering blooms, hoping to see us again but, unlike them, we never slept, or refreshed, nor returned.

I stand here at the gate as one of the billions of innocents who have faded from this place. I see the lonely, desperate figure rushing back to the sheds along the dusty road, hoping no one had spotted her feeble attempts. The trees share her deep despair. The force of the wind is pounding my face now as if I'm on a rollercoaster catapulting to its highest point, then plunging into despair. As despair is to slavery; as indifference is to farming; as human is to death; as autumn is to trees; as breath is to life; as voice is to sound; so anxiety is to freedom. I am a victim — but I'm also a victor. An angel appeared to me and shone their brilliance into the sheds. This story is our message-in-a-bottle, our letters to the angels.

Sweet is the voice of a sister in the season of sorrow.

— *Benjamin Disraeli*

Dear Dee,

Feeling dirty and dusty is not only good for the soul, it's just downright cleansing. Dust, dust, glorious dust! I'm watching you; slouched in your hammock, swaying side-to-side in pure relaxation as your thin auburn hair and the pages of the book you hold are flapping in the breeze. I'm enjoying the autumn sun too, remembering how my life was a dark, stark contrast a year ago today. Your tranquil state mirrors how I felt when we first met.

I was born into an unhappy, stressful, and violent environment, in a shed. I had two siblings: my brother, Rooney and sister, Henna. Absent fathers was the norm in this environment, and our mother wasn't in a good way when we were born: very weak and bruised. We were all removed from her as she couldn't take care of herself, let alone us. Unfortunately, we were all separated. We didn't know where each of the others had gone. What I do know, is that I went to hell and hoped and prayed that my siblings went to better homes than I had.

I wept thinking about them, but my cries were exacerbated by the agonising and deliberate searing of almost half of my nose. I was just a baby. Why was I disfigured so young? Who decided that my young, perfect body should be mutilated? I couldn't eat properly for many days after because my nose was so raw and sensitive. This is the earliest memory of my dysfunctional childhood. Days rolled into weeks, then into months. Then, after many months, I was moved to another home; an unloved orphan being shunted to the next place.

My eyes bulged when I arrived at yet another shed. Wow, so many orphans! Really? Were we all unwanted? Were their mothers also sick and unable to look after them? I looked around and discovered that they were all like me – mutilated orphans. Somehow this was comforting, and yet so overwhelming.

"Oh no, I've just wet myself!" I'd shriek every time. Not only did I wet myself every day, I used to crap myself too. I'd screech and flap around to divert attention from what I'd just done, because I was so embarrassed. Soiling myself may have been a psychological response to my situation but, the truth is, there were no sanitary facilities. Truly. I longed to be cleaned and clean.

"I stink. Poo and pee everywhere. Fuck, I hate being filthy," I'd scream, "I want a bath – dust, dust, glorious dust!"

To relieve my aching body, I'd try to stretch upwards and outwards but to do so would violate the space of someone else. Living with rows and rows of residents in confined, dark, and airless spaces created bitter, twisted residents who competed for everyday basics. We bickered all day long, scratching each other in frustration, unable to complain for help or change the situation ourselves. What's more, the floors were unevenly netted and sloped, and like a bad landlord, the Farmer Queen did nothing to fix it. They didn't care. No-one cared. My feet were deformed and blistered and my legs were riddled with arthritis.

"Fuck, I hate living here. This is no life." I'd scorn. Being stuck in poverty, unable to escape plunged me into a depression as dark as the room I lived in. As I witnessed what was happening to me and around me, I died a slow death in body and in spirit.

Giving birth in this environment was joyless. I laboured alone in a crowded space. My thoughts drifted to my mother; did she experience the same lonely, uncaring labour and delivery? All the while, I was being monitored and no sooner had I delivered, my babies would be gathered up. I was now my mother. My body wilted, too frail to move. Pathetic. How do you come back from such a shitty experience? I'd get high on the ammonia that choked the air to anaesthetise my pain. I felt nothing. My spirit had left me.

Whatever's done in the dark will always come to light. It was just another smelly, dark, gloomy night inside. As I was trying to get comfortable on the uneven and sloping floors, I heard voices. Not the usual whining, angry, anxious, desperate voices, but hopeful ones. Lights were darting to and fro, piercing the darkness as I hid my head in fear. The light show continued until one of the spotlights rested on me.

"Turn that off. Get it out of my face!" I screeched.

"Shhh," you whispered, "it's ok. Oh you poor little thing." You picked me up and caressed me, lightly stroking my head, and gently kissed my face with your pillowy lips. My anxiety relaxed. I felt your heartbeat and knew immediately: you had come with love. You weren't alone. You came with big brown cardboard boxes and friends with big beating hearts. It happened so fast. I found myself in one of those boxes. Despite my confusion, a sense of space and excitement took over, as if being stuffed into a spacious box was a good thing! I was barely alive as you carried my scrawny, crippled body out into the dead of night and loaded me into a van.

I rode in that box mentally, emotionally, spiritually, and physically broken and my liberation was just as traumatic. We arrived to your home in the foothills of the ranges; a sanctuary, my forever home. I tried not to become bitter, but everyone I'd cared about, my family and babies, were taken away from me, so liberation was bittersweet. I had nobody except you — the kind girl who, instead of staying home, snuggled up with her boyfriend in front of the TV, chose to come out in the cold autumn darkness, risking her own liberties to give me mine. I'd lost a lot, but gained a lot in you, my friend.

It was a mild Sunday afternoon, when a large white van drove up our leafy driveway. The driver flung open the side door and I instantly recognised the brown cardboard boxes within.

"What's this Dee? What's happening Dee?" I flapped excitedly.

"Out of the way," you commanded. You and your friends carried those boxes of scrawny, barely-alive, crippled bodies out of the van and into freedom. Been there, done that. I kept my distance and let you all tend to the rescued. I busied myself cleaning the yard, momentarily watching you and your friends resettle the new residents.

The next day, as I was taking a walk with my friends, I stopped in my tracks. Like a dog who hears the voice of their owner returning home at the end of the day, my heart leapt and body froze with surprise and anticipation.

"Henna, is that you?" I murmured at first, "Henna, is that you?!" I shouted. I ran towards the voice.

"Henna, it's me! Henna. It's me. Hendra!" I flapped around with all the eagerness of a dog about to go for a walk. Henna was grossly overweight and lethargic. When she saw me, she blinked and blinked at me.

"Yes Henna, it's me."

She struggled to stand because of the excess weight her skinny little legs couldn't withstand.

"Don't worry Henna. Don't stand. Just relax. You're safe now." I stayed with Henna and helped nurse her back to health.

"You're such a loving girl. Thanks for being so caring," you'd say. Dee, you weren't to know that we were separated siblings.

"Henna, when you're ready, you can tell me your story," I whispered. My sister was more traumatised than I was and while I was curious to know her story, part of me was afraid to know her truth. The truth is, none of us escapes childhood unscathed and Henna and I were no exception. As time passed, her deformities corrected themselves, she lost weight, her breathing improved, her heart began functioning normally and her eyes came alive. But there are still times when she just looks at me and calls my name —

"Hendra, Hendra," - then goes silent. She looks at me, repeats my name and goes silent. I let out a whimper every time. As her unofficial physiotherapist, personal trainer, and psychologist, we'd walk around the yard stretching, sunbathing, inhaling and exhaling the fresh clean air, and of course, indulging in dust baths.

Time heals a broken heart and body.

"Hendra, I don't want to talk about it, but only to say that my body meant more to others than my own life, but my life mattered to me so much more than my sickly body that I kept myself alive. Waiting, dreaming, hoping for salvation."

"It's ok Henna," I reply, "we don't have to talk about it." She actually continued.

"I lived in an overcrowded space made worse by the fact that we were all so obese, because the only food available was literally poison. I was drugged with arsenic and antibiotics to accelerate weight gain, like a paedophile grooming its young victim with sweets and pretty dresses for D-day. I struggled to stand, let alone move, eat, and drink but I willed myself, stepping over others and pushing my way through to reach the food and those damn water nozzles. I hated doing it, but I wanted to live."

"Oh my gosh, how awful. You're a very strong girl, Henna."

"The lights were always on, it never went dark and the constant unnatural light hurt my eyes. Hendra, this one day, a shadow blocked the light. I looked up and saw salvation. She reached down and picked me up and carried me out of that crowded, noisy, smelly, light-filled room and into the unknown. I squinted in the natural sunlight and gagged on the crisp air but the love I felt from the woman carrying me was overwhelming. Someone called out, "Kate put her in this box" My angel had a name. She also had warm brown eyes that eased my confusion. Kate placed in me a box and the next thing I know, I'm here."

"Well thank god for that!" I exclaimed, "I know that Kate and Dee are close friends and regularly rescue poor souls like us! You're right, they ARE angels."

Henna revealed, "My first night here was strangely dark, warm, clean and spacious. Everything I'd wished for. When everyone had gone to bed, I gazed out the window at the star-speckled sky and prayed: Thank you for bringing me here, from that cramped prison to this spacious home. Thank you''

"Amen to that sis. You're here now Henna, with me. Be happy."

Henna's story made me appreciate you so much more Dee. I'm defrosting from a past of cruel hardship and am now living as my true self: curious, fun-loving, sociable and caring. My life is as precious to me as it is to you. It meant nothing to the others back there in hell, but you've given me a life I love. Dust, dust, glorious dust! You've restored my spirit and my sister. Thank you Dee. Thank you for liberating my voice. I still curse and swear unashamedly but it's different this time;

"Fuck, I love my life!" Do you hear the difference?! That's my Voice.

Love you lots,

Hendra

When one realizes that his life is worthless he either commits suicide or travels.

— *Edward Dahlberg*

Dear Young Man,

I was in the midst of a mystery journey and meeting you certainly disrupted it! Neither exciting nor adventurous, this was a journey I had to endure like a long road trip with annoying siblings cramped in the back, listening to dad's replays of *I did it my way*. It was so stuffy in the back, made worse by the deafening music and stinky cigarette smoke polluting our oxygen. It was a very long journey, with no rest stops. Exhausted and thirsty, our paths collided rather than crossed. I write to you young man; a stranger who created this much-needed rest stop.

"Where are you? Come here, come on. Latch on. Here you go. Stop squabbling. Don't bite. Suck. Please come and drink. I can't help you. You have to help yourself. Come on. Drink my lovelies. Suck."

This was my desperate daily mantra from a bleak windowless shed, with walls of locked up words and cries from all those stuck within. I was disabled, unable to stand. Trapped. My babies had to use their natural instincts to search for my breasts and suckle, which was a huge relief as I couldn't help them. I'd cry for days when one of them couldn't feed themselves, and could do nothing as they'd become weak, starve, and die. There was no one around to help. My imposed quadriplegia restricted my movements. I struggled to scream but I couldn't make a sound. Nobody cared about me and my babies. I hated being restrained. I longed to search for my own food rather than being fed a daily diet of tasteless grains, which I would gobble up anyway in hungry surrender. Some days I wished I was dead, but then who would feed my babies? To alleviate my boredom and frustration, I'd sleep and dream that I was free, playing with my babies outside, foraging and exploring somewhere in the unknown outdoors where it was warm and safe. I was at peace when I slept. But then, I would wake up to a lifetime in detention.

Only a few weeks after their birth, my babies were taken from me to join a generation of stolen babies. That was it. A few weeks of hoping they'd suckle and survive and then they were gone. Just like that. It was one of the mysteries of life that we never dared ask about. I was so heavy with grief and upset that suicide became very appealing. After my most recent loss, Mr. Farrow decided I finally deserved a holiday. A permanent holiday, away from here. "You're done now, time to move on," Mr. Farrow announced.

"Done," he said. "Done." I said.

What does that even mean?

"Well about bloody time," I fumed, "how much more can a mother take?" There's nothing wrong with my body but how others see it. Mr. Farrow had abused yet safeguarded my body for his own gains. Enough was enough. I looked forward to my mystery journey, that everyone goes on after they're "done." I hoped it'd be relaxing.

Being upright and moving sent me into a spin like an elderly centurion on party drugs. My body ached all over as I made my way outside to a strange place I'd never been.

Covered in goosebumps, I was scared yet excited to see the mysterious outdoors. Besides being in physical pain, I was mentally furious at the unfairness of my situation. Like a child discovering the world, I looked up in wonder to see puffs of white candy-floss against a vivid blue background. I inhaled the fresh air like a newborn's first breath upon entering the outside world. A warm feeling came over me, but my curiosity was very brief as I was ushered directly from the indoors to another indoors, with wheels under it.

"What the hell is this? At least it has natural light."

It had grey stainless steel walls with large holes along the length of it. Hundreds of us crammed in together like trash in the back of a rubbish truck, a mass of pale flesh on a road-trip. It was uncomfortable, knocking against each other and suffocating in each other's heavy exhales. The cold steel walls became searing hot plates in the mid-afternoon sun. My muscles and joints ached as I started shaking and shivering. Almost passing out, I visualised being submerged in a mud bath, cooling down and relaxing.

"Oh, that would be heavenly," I gasped. Panting with a dry mouth, I manoeuvred myself to one of the large peep-holes, peering outside to catch a breath of air and a glimpse of the mysterious outdoors.

"Wow, it's so beautiful!" I marvelled at the laser-like sun rays glistering through the emerald pine forest that lined the path to our mystery destination. Despite being desperately hot and thirsty, my hopelessness lifted, basking in Mother Nature's glory.

Finally we arrived, but as soon as we came to a halt, a

crowd of people rushed towards us. I got spooked and pulled away from the peep-hole. They reached through the large peep-holes with water bottles, encouraging us to drink. And then I saw you. Twenty-something, male, unshaven, short army cut, dark blue eyes and bad body odour! I have a keen sense of smell and could tell that you'd been sweating in that scorching sun for a long while. You peered through the peep-hole and we locked eyes. You saw me. You actually saw me.

"Here, drink. Have a drink. Here you go. Drink," you beckoned. I drank greedily hoping you wouldn't stop watering me.

"Please stay," I grunted desperately.

Thank you, young man. Water had never tasted so good than that which was given with kindness. Nourishing and life-giving, it certainly quenched me.

Soon after, a commotion erupted. "Get away from there you bloody losers. Stop poisoning them! One day you're gonna get hurt and I'll be laughing!" The driver protested. Poison? It was just frickin' water. Poison was our special diet of tasteless grains dished out every day. Even more puzzling was your apology as you were leaving,

"I'm so sorry. You don't deserve this. Sorry."

Who was this young man? Why was he apologising? How did he know what I've been through? What's more, how did he just happen to be there, at that place, with water bottles? My questions were unsettling. I was so confused, yet somewhat hopeful that there may be others like you who know the truth. I watched you retreat across the road, looking sad. I wanted to hug you and run away with you. I imagined freedom with my knight in shining armour — exploring the emerald pine forest together and basking in the sunshine while getting a back massage! As with sleep, I woke up to reality.

My journey's almost over now, as the engine has restarted and Frank Sinatra's *I did it my way* is playing yet again. I can see enormous barbed-wire gates opening, welcoming us into a complex of buildings with huge chimneys. I hope there are grassy areas here to wander and till the soil.

Goodbye, Young Man. I hope your life is as big and bold as your heart. Your water changed everything. Thank you for seeing me: a Voiceless.

Love,

Pink

The healthy man does not torture others –
generally it is the tortured who turn into torturers.

Carl Jung

My Darling Jane,

You must have nine lives because you keep bouncing in and out of that court room victorious! You keep me on my knees every time girl - thank God my prayers are always answered. I dreamt about you last night, so I got up to write to you before sunrise.

I've watched you grow into a beautiful, strong-willed, intelligent, compassionate woman who's always had my back when your father, Fred, was unkind to me. You always stood up for me. One of the most difficult times of my life was when he sent you away to boarding school. Why did he do that? There was a perfectly good private school just down the road, but he sent you away. Far away from me. I sobbed for weeks remembering the giggly little girl who would keep me company in the fields, read to me, brush my hair, and perform short plays and songs for me. My heart ached for you. I loved roaming freely and exploring the outdoors but I couldn't go outside much. I was kept busy. Life on the farm was unrelenting. I wished I could've spent more time with friends but I never had a chance, which saddened me. But I always had you. You had time for me. You were different. I wasn't just a number. I was *Daisy* to you.

Do you remember when you and I used to play hide-and-seek around the trees next to the old barn? Your laughter and playfulness filled my heart with joy. I loved it when you used to practice your flute. I'd sit and listen with the love and patience of a passionate music teacher as you tried to perfect my favourite Mozart tunes. Your soft jaw and small lips produced beautiful music as your sandy-blonde ponytail bounced to the rhythm. Our games and your music lifted my spirits which were, more often than not, depressed.

Last week, Fred was orienting a new female worker. "Ready!" Fred announced. "Ready…?" she said, unsure of what was about to happen. Hearing this drained the blood from my face as a scene which has harrowed me for years played out in my head. Fred was calling for me from the sheds so we stopped playing hide-and-seek to heed his call.

"Jane, go and do your homework and get ready for dinner," he ordered, "and shut the door behind you." Goosebumps covered me like a rash as the door slowly closed behind your exit. It was Frisky Fred Time again, as my top half was tied to a rack and I was left anxiously waiting, anticipating a fate so dreadful, I started trembling.

"Now just relax. It won't hurt. It'll all be over before you know it, if you don't move," he'd command. My muscles tensed as his rough leathery hands inspected my body, and then with a slap on my backside, he said, "Ready!" I floated into a trance, refusing to be in that moment, that is, until you burst into the room, shrieking like a wounded cockatoo caught in a trap.

"What are you doing daddy? What are you doing? Stop it. Stop it! Leave her alone!" Your screams jolted me back to the present moment and I pulled away as best I could

— but I was stuck. Your purity punctuated the darkness in that room. In his fury, Fred picked you up with his strong broad arms and threw you out but you got back up and ran back into the room, hitting and kicking your father with all the energy a five year old could muster. The bulging veins on Fred's neck almost burst as he picked you up again and shook you violently. I rattled the rack angrily.

"No Fred, stop, stop. Don't hurt her. Don't hurt her!" I watched your head and limbs flopping to and fro until he abruptly stopped and held you up to his face, threatening,

"That's enough Jane." "You're a bad man daddy."

And with that, he literally tossed you out again and slammed the door behind him. His heavy brow bone frowned with anger and his flushed red face matched mine. I was a distressed mess of helplessness, sobbing uncontrollably, not for myself, but for you my darling Jane. I was embarrassed that you had seen me at my most vulnerable and frustrated, that I couldn't protect you and me against the evil that was your father. I'm sorry you had to see that. I'm sorry you had to experience what no child should ever have to experience. Indeed, this could've damaged you but it didn't, it hasn't. You're an angelic warrior my Jane.

As you know, nine months after that dramatic event, I gave birth to my fourth child – a beautiful baby boy; Bobby. You were there when he was born and in the midst of my loud groaning and pushing a watermelon out of my arse, I heard your excited elation when he emerged into the world.

"Yay it's a boy, my new friend!" you exclaimed, jumping

up and down. Fred, on the other hand, frowned with the disappointment of a father who'd just received yet another son after expecting a daughter. You couldn't understand why Fred was unhappy but no one really understood him anyhow. Fred didn't allow me to feed Bobby. My full breasts leaked and I needed relief.

"Please give some to my baby," I pleaded.

"I don't know why you bother asking, Daisy," Fred scoffed.

"Daddy you have to give some to Bobby or he'll starve!"

"Stop calling it Bobby," Fred said pointing at him, "this isn't a game Jane."

Fred had my breasts expressed and sold my milk to the market, while Bobby had milk formula.

"Jane, I swear, you're not my daughter." I wholeheartedly agreed.

You were Bobby's best friend and big sister. He'd wriggle his little body back and forth excitedly whenever he heard your voice or saw you. He wanted to play! But I'm sure you remember the day when you, Bobby and I were enjoying the warm sunshine, and two men visited. I grabbed Bobby and took off.

"What's wrong Daisy? Why are we running?" I'm sorry I scared you but I was scared too at that moment. I had already lost three other babies.

Fred was calling, "Jane, where is he?"

You were panting breathlessly alongside me.

"Daisy what's wrong?" I pinned Bobby between myself and the large pine tree at the top of the small hill where we used roll the ball. At that moment, Fred and the two men had reached us.

"C'mon girl, stand aside. Jane go home. C'mon, let's not a make scene you two." The men tried to get around me to take my boy; I pushed them away with all my might. My heart was racing a marathon as a rowdy scuffle ensued and all the while, I could hear you shouting at Fred,

"No Daddy, no!" Losing his patience, one of the men pulled out his 45mm.

"Fred, your daughter's getting out of hand. Deal with her." Fred seized you. The second man grabbed hold of me while the man with the gun pulled my Bobby away. As I was body-slamming the man holding me, I saw you break free of Fred's grip. He reached out to snag your ponytail but you sprinted away.

"Yes!" I cheered.

Bobby was crying out for us as you were running after them.

"Go Jane. Get him!" I yelled. You caught up to them and began launching your signature hitting and kicking so he'd let go of Bobby.

Bang. A gunshot to the head ceased all protests. I slumped to the ground wailing and your piercing cries, I will never forget. We were left behind to grieve in defeat as they continued to load the truck and head to market. I clutched my chest as if the bullet had punctured it and you suffered the same distress. I was never the same after that day and neither were you, my beautiful Jane.

"I love you Daisy. I hate daddy," you whispered as we consoled each other in a tight embrace.

When you turned seven, Fred decided to break us up. He chose to get rid of you rather than me, as I was worth more to him. The truth is, I paid for your private school fees. The day you left, my heart was heavy and toxic like lead. I wanted to slaughter myself - my life was nothing without you in it. I'd already lost four babies and now I was about to lose you. Fred had always held our fate in his deranged hands. Upon leaving, you kissed me.

"I love you Daisy. I'm going away, but I'll be back." And you were. I looked forward to the school holidays as much as teachers did. Every school holiday you returned like an angel appearing to a desperate person in need. Life with Fred continued – forced impregnation, stealing my children and milk for profit - but at least you weren't around to witness it. I didn't care, as long as you were safe, away from this violent hell hole. I enjoyed your visit yesterday and as always, I felt like I was at my own funeral when you left.

"Goodbye, mum. My own mum ran away when I was a baby but you've always been here for me, and you never gave up your own babies. You're my mum. I know your life hasn't been easy but I'm going to help others like you." Your words reminded me why I love you so much yet at the same time, I felt anxious for you and your future, which would be anything but mediocre!

I'm playing our song *Concerto for Flute and Harp* in my head as I write, imagining what's in front of us as being bigger and better than what's behind us. It's almost sunrise and Raymond Rooster will soon herald in a new day. I'm retiring today. I'm tired and spent. I can't give anymore and as I approach my end, I lament my four lost babies and above all, you, my darling Jane: the warrior, the defender of me and all future me's; the Voiceless.

Live well, my angel voice. Stay safe.

Love,

Daisy

Freedom is never voluntarily given by the oppressor; it must be demanded by the oppressed.

Martin Luther King Jr.

Dear Teenager,

I don't know why or how you knew, but you were the superhero I'd always wanted to meet! Before I go on my big overseas adventure, here's my story, which you enabled.

Wanted.

I was wanted and lovingly conceived in a laboratory tray. Science did its magic and ta-da: I was created! Actually, a community of us was created and we grew up together. After successful embryonic incubation, I was transferred to another facility, where I stayed until I fully matured. I wasn't alone even though I didn't have live parents; I was part of a parentless community. We were all special indeed.

As we were growing up in a huge glass tank, Sammi and I became close friends, looking out for each other. Despite the overcrowded living conditions, we found opportunities to play and cure our boredom but one day, I lost her in a game of catch. My heart beat faster than a rapid jack-hammer.

"Sammi, where are you?"

I looked across the glass wall to see the Farmer Queen weighing and measuring her, and giving her an injection. I didn't know we were having medical check-ups. Next minute, it was my turn. Everyone had to go through the same procedure and it became a regular routine thereafter. Many didn't like being poked and prodded and became aggressive.

"Sal, everyone's getting bigger now, surely they're going to give us a bigger space to live in? Everyone's getting frustrated and short-tempered."

"They don't mean to be like that Sammi but you're right, we're like moving sardines in a can and we ain't sardines!"

"Stay close to me Sammi, there's a lot of aggro and bullying happening. Stay close."

Soon after, we were all moved to the seaside. How wonderful to be outdoors! But there were no sea views, beach walks, or rolling waves onto the shore. It was a netted sea enclosure. We just went round and round and round, going nowhere.

Caught.

Our new home demonstrated that better isn't always good.

I loved swimming. I yearned to swim far beyond the peninsula heads but wasn't allowed to. Perhaps they feared I wouldn't return. They were right!

"Sal, take me away from here. Let's go. I've got a bad feeling," whispered Sammi.

"Like what? Have you seen something? Heard something?"

"I overhead others saying that we're gonna get separated soon and I don't want that. Who's gonna look after me? My back's getting worse. It's so painful now. Sal, can we leave?"

"Wait. I'll look into it."

I went round and round and round but couldn't find a way out. I had never felt as entrapped as I did at that moment. Sammi was relying on me, but I couldn't find an escape exit.

"Sammi eat. You need to eat." I urged.

"I can't eat this crap anymore. It's not healthy but we've got no choice," she'd snap, "I swear, our poor diet and housing have caused my back problems." She was convinced of this. She'd go on and on and on about how unnatural the food was, containing a porridge mixture of sardines, food colouring, antibiotics and fish oil. To make matters worse, many others were getting sick too, further supporting her theory.

"What's wrong mate?" I asked another. "Lice."

Sammi screamed, "See, see what did I tell you? We've got lice now because we're living in jam-packed, stuffy conditions. I want out of here before I catch it."

One by one, the afflicted died. This was no ordinary lice; it was an invasion of ravenous vampire lice. The final straw was the Farmer Queen's efforts to destroy the lice. A new community, similar to us, arrived to remove the lice. They particularly loved eating lice, picking them off us and devouring them. Yuck! Each to their own I suppose. But now our living space had become even tighter. Enough was enough. We had to get out of there. It became stressful and I lost my appetite, as did Sammi.

One afternoon, Sammi squealed: "OMG Sal, look, look what they've done to Sienna!" They'd slither open, gutted her, and tossed her aside — still conscious. We watched on like a horror movie as they systematically picked out more victims from my community. Then another was bashed over the head while still struggling to breathe. I was watching my own death.

"Quick Sammi, hide. Move it." We hid at the deep rear of our enclosure, luckily escaping the first round as night fell and operations ceased. Thank goodness.

"Oh Sal, we're not special at all. We were all born to be slaughtered. Is this how it's meant to be?" She cried all night while I brainstormed how I was going to hatch an escape. Later that evening, you; the Teenager, appeared like the angel to Mary in order to save her newborn son, Jesus, from King Herod's slaughter fest.

I was awoken to the sound of your slashing. The netted walls were coming down. The heavens were opening with welcoming freshness. I could breathe and move freely. You had slashed enough to allow young and old to escape. I suddenly became scared, hesitating to leave the enclosure I craved to leave. Then you saw me. Your large grey eyes widened.

"Go, go, get out of here, hurry."

I turned to Sammi. "Let's go now, everyone's leaving, this is our chance, c'mon!"

"I'm afraid Sal. What's out there? I heard it's polluted, wild and unfriendly."

"I can't believe you're hesitating Sammi. This is what you've wanted for so long. I've been sick to death of listening to your constant grumblings about how bad it's been and now that you've got a chance to escape this, you're worried about a little pollution?!"

I looked up at your puzzled face, confused that we were still hanging around squabbling while almost everyone had gone.

Weeeooo weeeooo weeeooo weeeooo weeeooo!

"Guys, I'm going, the alarm's just gone off. Go, go now. Go live the life you're meant to live." And you sprinted off.

"Sammi come with me. I'll take care of you as I've always done. Let's go."

At that moment, loud angry voices echoed and all the lights came on.

"I'm going. Are you coming?" I begged.

"Look, there are still a few here," someone shouted. "You go Sal. Go. I'm staying. Go Sal."

And without another moment's thought, I torpedoed out of there. Alone. I wept as I was escaping. Leaving Sammi behind shredded my heart. Her fear of the unknown had paralysed her. I was so angry with her, yet so sad for my friend. I would've taken care of her and her spinal problems. Did she doubt me? When I was a safe distance away I looked back, sobbing with mixed emotions. Freedom was traumatic. A single light blinked in the darkness like an emerging pimple on the surface. It was now a place of no return and my friend Sammi was there, far away from me. I turned around, tears flooding my eyes, and fled to the headlands. Bye bye Sammi.

Thank you, Teenager. Thank you for cutting me free, enabling me to embark on this adventure that is life. So far, I've met many who are similar to me and a diversity of others, especially in colouring. I think Sammi's obsession with being fed food colouring may have been correct?! I'm off to different waters now, to discover the world as I'm compelled to migrate. I remember what you said that night and I will "live the life I was meant to live." Thank you Teenager, whoever you are and wherever you are, stay fearless and continue doing good deeds for those like me – the Voiceless.

Much Love and Farewell,

Sal

It takes a great deal of bravery to stand up to our enemies, but just as much to stand up to our friends.

J. K. Rowling

My Dearest Friend,

We only met once for a very short time, but that one moment in time has remained with me until now. I had just become a new mum having given birth to twins: a boy and a girl. The indescribable pain which almost exploded my insides instantly subsided when I pushed out those little bundles of innocence, whose wide, curious eyes met mine upon entering the warm, inviting surrounds. Unlike the other mothers, I was spoilt. There's something about twins that attracts double attention and double accolades, which was lucky for me! It was bitterly cold outside so I really appreciated the indoor warmth. Of course you wouldn't have known, but I had already lost three babies in similar, harshly cold conditions so yes, I was feeling special indeed. My twins were spared the rough weather and food scarcity because their lives mattered in a way which was a mystery to me.

A few days later, as I was grooming my babies, a group of men were circulating, doing their rounds and inspecting all us mothers and our newborns. I noticed you amongst them. I mean to say, who wouldn't notice you in your expensive, red Italian coat! The others didn't address or acknowledge me, but you did.

"Hello. What beautiful wee ones you have there." Your kind hazel eyes warmed my heart, which was already full with pride and happiness. The others talked over me, they were more interested in my babies, but not in the same way that you were. Perhaps your smile was the difference. The Farmer Queen stepped forward and I stepped back timidly. I naturally get nervous and flighty when people get too close.

I was introduced to the group. "This is Sheila. She's done very well for us." Another person from the group leaned forward and picked up my baby boy. Was he concerned about something? I wondered. I looked up at him waiting for an explanation but he proceeded to walk away with my baby. Nothing was said. I ran to the door.

"Wait, what's happening?" Silence.

"Where is he taking him?" you asked. The group laughed at you as if you had just asked the most stupid question ever. I watched you retreat to the back of the group like a lost sheep rejoining the flock. I felt sorry for you but, I needed you to stand up to them, to find out where they were taking my baby. But you didn't. I protested loudly, thrashing around the warm comfortable confines which had suddenly become cold and frightening. The pain of losing another baby was unbearable. I began smashing my head against the wall.

"I can't take this anymore!" No one noticed. No one cared.

The group resumed their rounds as I continued my insane head-banging.

"I want my baby back! Bring him back!" I howled, but my cries were ignored. That is, until my pounding head hit a soft palm of kindness. You softened my blows with your delicate hand as my head and heart were throbbing with pain. I looked up at you and our teary eyes met in solidarity.

"Please go, run, go find my baby and bring him back to me," I begged.

"I'm so sorry. I'm sorry about your baby," you whispered, gently clasping my head.

"Sorry about what? Please don't be sorry. Don't be shy. Do something!"

My body shook with fear and anger but you quietened my pain even if just for that brief moment.

"I have to go now but I promise, I'll make this right for all of you. One day. I promise." And with that sincere declaration, you were gone.

I watched you scurry away to rejoin the group and I immediately grabbed my baby girl who'd been scared into a corner, cowering at the sight of her mother acting wild and crazy. I comforted her, and she, me.

I think about you often my friend, whoever you are. The girl in the expensive red Italian coat with the big heart, kind hazel eyes and soft delicate hands. You lightened my darkness with your whispers of empathy. My second twin was also taken shortly after you and your group had left. I fretted so badly; I overheated and threw up. Alone, lonely and stressed, my head hung as low as it could drop. I wanted to self-exterminate, to end the pain. As I slept, I would hear their innocent cries and see their sweet, perfect faces in my dreams. One morning, their cries became deafening as I was awoken to their return.

"Oh my babies. You're back!" I cried, hugging them like a

loved one returning from war. I squeezed them so tightly not wanting to let go. Yet something was different. Terror washed over me in a frantic nano-second, thinking that these weren't my babies. I instantly inspected their little bodies and discovered they'd been mutilated in the rear end.

"My poor babies. What monsters did this?" I wept, "Why? Why do they have to do this? Perfect one day, then maimed the next." Their rear ends were still sensitive, red, and excruciatingly sore. They were unsteady on their feet. My tears flowed as I watched them shake and stumble. I believed we were special being inside, sheltered from the merciless cold outdoors but now, it proved to be equally merciless inside the deceptive warmth.

As the weather improved we ventured outside, resuming a seemingly normal life in the sunlit buttercup fields. It was Easter, so they said, and everyone seemed to be in good spirits.

"It's a good year!" the Farmer Queen said. Rex, the over-enthusiastic Border Collie was on a mission that day. His presence always unsettled me, so I'd run away and keep my distance. Rex loved managing everybody but despite his bossiness, I always knew he had my back and would never allow anything bad happen to me or my babies.

On this particular day, hardworking Rex escorted us into an enclosed area with the time and tension of an Olympic runner in their final 10 metres. But then I was separated from the twins. I called out to Rex,

"Where are all the young ones going?" "It's Easter. It's all good," he shouted.

And that was that. Gone. Whatever Easter is, it's got my babies and all the other babies. I paced back and forth in the enclosure and couldn't bring myself to imagine what Easter was, or what Easter did with all the babies. It was so noisy, Rex barking orders against the bleating of scared babies and anxious mothers.

"What are you doing for Easter? Who are you spending it with?"

Judging from everyone's demeanour, Easter was a happy time, but for me, it was as if someone had pierced my side with a sword and I had died, never to rise. No miracle or celebrations for me.

It's been just over a year since our brief encounter but many times, I needed the comfort of your soft hands. I haven't forgotten your pure kindness. You heard me. I hope that you've found the confidence to shine your light for everyone to see and to speak up with courage. I'm positively certain that you're keeping your promise to me; a Voiceless

Love,

Sheila

Truth does not sit in a cave and hide like a lie. It wanders around proudly and roars loudly like a lion.

Suzy Kazzem

To my Voiceless Friend,

You may think that your cries fall upon deaf ears, but they don't. We hear you. We're fighting for you. Your letter warmed my broken heart. Broken for you, my friend.

My lone confinement is for you. These prison walls are tired and scream of past souls pondering their existence. Like you, I've lost my freedoms. I'm living the minimalist's life for the next eighteen months. The law protects the farm and its profitability. You and I are victims of the agribusiness cage but there's one distinction: I chose to be here, you didn't. You didn't choose this life. It's not a life. I hear you.

An animal's perpetual whining is an aural memory from my childhood. I'm a farm girl who loved the farm life growing up but, unlike my siblings, I became more and more uneasy as I grew older. As children, my two older brothers and I used to fish, trap, shoot, and knife anything that moved! Mum and Dad worked hard on the farm, diligently tending to the animals and the land like their lives depended on it — because it did. The farm was their livelihood; their whole life. We children had chores - not the city kind like washing dishes and cleaning your room; we had to tend to the 300-plus animals, prepare and distribute feed, clean the sheds and, of course, wash the dishes and clean our rooms! For the first twelve years of my life, I never realised or questioned why our female animals seemed happy one minute then upset the next. We ignored their persistent cries, overridden by the fact that their pain was my family's gain. Mum and Dad would celebrate their profits with more animals, a new piece of machinery, a home renovation, a new vehicle, or an overseas family holiday. Life was beautiful, until I was awoken by an unlikely friend.

"Why are you eating a pig?" Gary interrupted. "It's not pig," I snapped, "it's pork.'

"No it's not, that used to be a smart pig," he said, shaking his head.

"So what?"

Gary misinterpreted my *I don't care* response as; *Give me an explanation*!

"Pigs on farms live an awful life and don't get to stay with their mothers because they're taken away and killed, so that you can eat them in a sandwich."

"Go away. You're a real nutter."

On this particular day in grade 7, I'd met Gary, a pleasant yet somewhat awkward, brainy guy who delighted in commenting on my lunches. His hooked nose, thick wavy hair, fair freckled skin and lanky stature were the source of lighthearted ridicule. Despite our disagreements, Gary never gave up on me, insisting we should be friends and so it was. He grew on me. Every lunchtime, he would inspect my lunch:

"Fish fingers were once fish. Soon we're gonna run out

of fish because we're taking too many of them and we're destroying their homes, the oceans, lakes and rivers."

"Gosh Gary, just shut up and eat your lunch."

Gary packed his own lunchbox which was truly strange, but that was Gary; different. We became good friends and for a long time, I didn't invite him to my place because of my family's farming activities. But I couldn't avoid it any longer seeing as I'd been to his place many times and enjoyed time away from farm duties!

"Mum and Dad, can my friend Gary come to dinner at the weekend? I've been to his place lots of times so can he come over? Just once?"

"Is that the friend who hates meat and farmers? Is that wise? We're gonna have meat whether he likes it or not. He can come if he doesn't turn his nose up, otherwise I'll ask him to leave. Deal?"

"I guess so Dad."

I warned Gary about the carnivore menu and asked him to tone down the anti-meat comments. Of course, warnings are only successful if they're heeded.

"Help yourself Gary. There's baked sweet potatoes, broccoli with flaked almonds, Greek salad and garlic Brussels sprouts." I appreciated mum's efforts and so did Gary.

"So Gary," my father started, "you don't eat meat?"

My mouthful of sweet potato became chilli hot. I glared at Gary to go easy. But with the confidence of a young, mouthy, free-thinker, he replied, "No sir, I don't. I don't like the cruelty on farms every day and I feel bad for their suffering. I love animals so I don't eat them."

"Interesting Gary. Is that what your parents taught you?"

"No that's what I think. Mum and Dad are like you but one day, I hope they'll be like me."

My brothers laughed out loud with their unsightly mouthfuls. Gary's answer surprised all of us, most of all, me. At that moment, I wanted to be like him. Brave, self-assured and passionate. I wanted that. Dad drove Gary home and upon his return, declared,

"That boy's got a lot to learn about real life, but I admire his guts. His poor parents!" I went to bed and couldn't wait to see Gary again on Monday morning to begin my quest.

And that's what led me to this moment of confinement. At a young age, Gary helped me find my compassion. He opened my eyes to your value. I'm writing to you from this cage because I value you and your life. Many others don't. I love you to pieces but they love you in pieces. We have a different perspective and while I understand them, I categorically reject their beliefs, that is, their right to dominate and bully you; their right to rape and degrade you; their right to remove your children; their right to profit from your suffering; their right to deny you a long life; their right to kill you. If evil had a face, the faces of those who subscribe to these rights are a close fit. Lucifer dances with evil but not with me or others like me. We dance with our humanity, which Lucifer detests. My compassion had been frozen in the everyday grind of growing up on a farm, mindlessly accepting those evil rights.

As soon as we finished high-school, Gary and I put our savings together and bought ourselves Greyhound bus tickets to the big city with big dreams. We met like-minded people who danced to our tune and so it was; our lifelong advocacy work began. To lessen or eliminate your pain was and still is our mission.

I feel sick in the stomach thinking about the suffering you endure on farms every day and continue to call on fellow human beings to look within and recognise that there's something missing in their humanity, something they're not seeing, some kind of disconnect from their compassion. My wish is that one day soon, they'll move beyond their discomfort and go deeper to find the uncomfortable truth of where their food comes from, and why your body is as precious to you as theirs is to them. It's astonishing that many would rather sit with injustice than in discomfort. I disrupted their comfort and ended up here!

Please know that we're doing all we can to rescue you and to spread the message of your value and the injustices you experience. To disrupt the disconnect. You can't see us but we're working hard for you and sometimes we're just outside your gate, sending our love and sad apologies for your suffering. We protest outside farms and industry head offices; we hold silent vigils outside your windowless sheds; we enter farms and rescue some of you and take photos and videos of your miserable existence to share with the disconnected; we create powerful documentaries and publish books, magazines, newspaper articles, and pamphlets to educate and encourage cruelty-free living; we write submissions to government to improve welfare legislation; we protest against new factory farms opening up in our communities; we provide sanctuaries for those rescued; we fundraise to support our own advocacy and each other's. These and many other activities are all for you.

This is where we are, at this point in time. I know it can't happen fast enough for you all but please know, as sure as Black slavery ended in 19th century America when the majority of their society said it wouldn't happen, it couldn't happen; the end to animal farming will come. Millions of us live mindfully with you at the centre of our lifestyle. Eating a plant-based diet and using non-animal products has saved millions of you from harm. Even though you can't see or experience this in your own life, please know that we're making a difference to the lives of others like yourself and continue to chip away at the evil culture that profits from your reproductive system. It's a disgusting truth that in the 21st century, we're still enslaving and mistreating intelligent sentient beings like yourself for no good reason other than, "It tastes nice," and "I need the protein." It's a lie of course, as we can absolutely get our required protein needs from plants.

My parents visited this afternoon. A part of me died today. Mum cried into her cotton handkerchief, soaked after years of worry for a wayward daughter. The lines on their faces deepened with disappointment, but they still love me nonetheless, as I do them. Gary's parents eventually gave up eating animals, whereas mine continue to delight their taste buds in wilful ignorance. They know the smell of barbecued flesh better than they know lavender, mint, rhubarb, and oranges.

"You love these animals so much; you're willing to do jail time?" Mum cried.

"Yes I am. The law protects the cruel master. So, yes

I am." I hid my grin in my hands realising I was now the twelve-year-old kid who'd pledged to be like Gary, my lanky friend who'd become my hero. I was living my purpose.

I'm not an angel. I'm an ordinary human with an extraordinary perspective. I'm the so-called *crazy one* who's always angry about the covert cruelty that persists on farms every day. I'm so sorry for your pain. You don't deserve this. My heart aches for you. Honestly, I'm a little scared in this cage but your oppression is more important than my fear. Over the next eighteen months, my resolve will grow stronger as I plan a spectacular come-back in freedom! Unlike you, I live and make choices every day. I choose you. I'm not a mother myself but as a female, I share your desire for warm relationships and your fear of dying. You deserve to choose a partner, reproduce when and how you want, raise your children, socialise with friends, and you absolutely deserve to live to an old age.

Thank you for your letter. I've kissed it a thousand times, clutching it to my heart. I'm happy that I touched your life at one point in time but it still torments me to know that I can't shine a light on all of you. But we're trying. Believe me, we're trying. The twelve-year-old in me still sparkles and as she did then, I pledge to advocate for your freedoms for the rest of my life in the hope for a kinder world for you and your species and this planet that we share.

With much Love,

Peta

Your Voice

We can help the next generation, with the stories we write today.

Lailah Gifty Akita

My Dear Granddaughter,

My name is Bella and I am your mum's mother. We'll never meet, my darling granddaughter, because my time has come. It's terribly cold outside as the icy southern winds blow through the sheds. I can see my lift waiting to transport me to retirement where I'm promised eternal bliss. But before I go, I want to give you hope — because that's all I can give you at this moment.

My hope for you, my darling granddaughter, is that you have a voice. My generation whispers in the corners daring not to speak. We aren't even seen. We're invisible and mute. Life happens around us and we just march to the tune of the powerful and their mean, authoritarian voices. I hope that your life will be one that is loud and proud. I want you to find it, to guard it jealously, to use it, to share it. Stand in it bravely, my darling. Never let those mean and powerful voices silence you. Use your voice and your talents to help yourself and others achieve peace and justice. My wish for you is a free, happy, self-directed life.

My generation produces offspring as a career. But it doesn't have to be like that for you, my granddaughter. Protect your uterus. It's yours. You are its keeper. Ours were pimped continuously. I hope you'll be free to choose your partner one day. Someone who loves and desires you and your voice. Beware the suitor who seeks to crush that. If you decide to produce offspring, I hope you have a long life together, experiencing the precious wonders that only this bond can provide. Our offspring died very young and it's my hope that yours will survive to see out your senior years. Losing a life that came from within you is the most terrifying thing that could ever happen to a mother. No other loss compares. There are no words to describe that kind of pain. I hope you never suffer the losses of my generation.

So, my beautiful granddaughter, the time has come to leave my home. I'm being beckoned to take my place. Your mother is now living with another family who are rumoured to be ethical humanitarians. I hope they're kind to her and her offspring. I hope you're born into opportunity. Grab it my granddaughter. Create a life you love, which my generation could only dream of. Do it for yourself. Do it for us - the Voiceless.

Love,

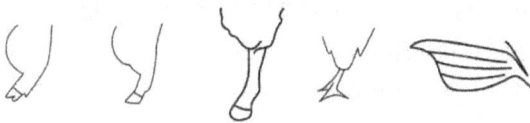

Grandma Bella

FROM the AUTHOR'S heart to YOURS

"Whatever's done in the dark will always come to light," my mother would say.

I knew what she meant. As a child, it meant that if I did something wrong that she wouldn't approve of, she'd find out about it, one way or another. And when she did find out, all hell would break loose, so it was just best to be honest and transparent. As an adult, the meaning has changed somewhat. Whatever wrong is committed in secrecy will be discovered and exposed, and all hell will break loose. This is the situation facing animal activists who dare to uncover the cruel and covert operations of animal agriculture and aquaculture businesses.

Animal activists are, more often than not, vilified by those industries that rely on the slavery of innocent, sentient beings to fund their lifestyle choices. Governments that rely on kick-backs from these industries support their calls to criminalise and imprison activists who attempt to rescue the abused and report on the abuse to the wider community. My mother was right. All hell is breaking loose. Animal activists are loosening the chains of farm animal slavery, thereby reducing the power of those who glean an income from the lives of these gentle, intelligent, virtuous beings.

I wrote this book in honour of the zillions of farm animals who suffer inhumane atrocities, and in honour of the animal activists who work tirelessly to bring the plight of farm animals to the light of day.

I dedicate it to Lucky; my canine son, friend and protector. My empathy and love for Lucky extends to all animals, domestic, farmed and wild. The intensity of this empathic love gives me the courage to speak out against the violent torture afflicted upon the powerless and voiceless farm animals.

I kissed a pig on her way to slaughter and I became hooked on seeking justice for her and sharing my love with all creatures. May you also become hooked on discovering the truth, and righting the wrongs of the farm animal holocaust.

Connect with me and share your insights as a vegan, animal lover and activist:

Email: suli@suliwrites.com

Website: www.suliwrites.com

Facebook: www.facebook.com/suli.autagavaia

Instagram: @suli.autagavaia

I'd welcome a Review of this book:

www.amazon.com/books